JUN 2 0 2017

12 FRIGHTENING TALES OF
ALIEN ENCOUNTERS

by Brandon Terrell

STORY
LIBRARY

www.12StoryLibrary.com

12-Story Library is an imprint of Peterson Publishing Company and Press Room Editions.

Produced for 12-Story Library by Red Line Editorial

Photographs ©: ElvisFontenot/iStockphoto, cover, 1; Elena Schweitzer/Shutterstock Images, 4, 28; Public Domain, 5; Bettmann/Corbis, 6, 8, 10; Mike Redwine/Shutterstock Images, 7; powerofforever/iStockphoto, 9; Orhan Cam/Shutterstock Images, 13; AP Images, 14; IAU and Sky & Telescope Magazine, 15; Potapov Alexander/Shutterstock Images, 16; Fedor Selivanov/Shutterstock Images, 17; US Department of Defense, 18; Johns Hopkins University/APL/NASA, 19; TVJunkie/Bass-Strasse.png, 21; Ed Kolenovsky/AP Images, 23; Ursatii/Shutterstock Images, 25, 29; M & Y News Ltd./Rex Features/AP Images, 26; Parker Haeg/Demotix/Demotix/Corbis, 27

Library of Congress Cataloging-in-Publication Data
Names: Terrell, Brandon, 1978- author.
Title: 12 frightening tales of alien encounters / by Brandon Terrell.
Other titles: Twelve frightening tales of alien encounters
Description: North Mankato, MN : 12-Story Library, [2017] | Series: Scary and
    spooky | Audience: Grades 4 to 6. | Includes bibliographical references
    and index.
Identifiers: LCCN 2016002349 (print) | LCCN 2016009354 (ebook) | ISBN
    9781632352934 (library bound : alk. paper) | ISBN 9781632353436 (pbk. :
    alk. paper) | ISBN 9781621434597 (hosted ebook)
Subjects: LCSH: Human-alien encounters--Juvenile literature. | Unidentified
    flying objects--Juvenile literature. | Curiosities and wonders--Juvenile
    literature.
Classification: LCC QB54 .T47 2017 (print) | LCC QB54 (ebook) | DDC
    001.942--dc23
LC record available at http://lccn.loc.gov/2016002349

Printed in the United States of America
Mankato, MN
May, 2016

Access free, up-to-date content on this topic plus a full digital version of this book. Scan the QR code on page 31 or use your school's login at 12StoryLibrary.com.

Table of Contents

A Saucer Hovers Over Los Angeles

On February 25, 1942, at 2:00 a.m., air raid sirens and antiaircraft fire cut through the calm sky around Los Angeles, California. Searchlights arced across the clouds. Flashes of light from gunfire glowed like fireworks. The Battle of Los Angeles had begun.

The United States entered World War II (1939–1945) weeks after the bombing of Pearl Harbor, Hawaii. The country was not prepared for another attack. The military took immediate action when an unidentified object

It is unclear what was in the sky the night of the Battle of Los Angeles.

1,440
Estimated rounds of ammunition fired by the military at the unidentified object.

- The sighting occurred on February 25, 1942, several months after the attack on Pearl Harbor.
- The object was a pale orange color and moved slowly over Los Angeles, California.
- Antiaircraft weapons were fired at the object.
- The only damage came from traffic accidents.

The United States was on high alert after the bombing at Pearl Harbor.

was seen over the city.

Eyewitnesses claimed to see a large, pale orange object hovering and moving slowly over the sky. Antiaircraft weapons were fired. Nothing stopped the object. Though it appeared to be hit, it remained undamaged.

The shooting stopped at dawn. The mysterious aircraft was nowhere to be seen. No major damage had

taken place in Los Angeles. But many minor traffic incidents were reported. There had also been one death. Someone suffered heart failure because of the excitement.

Newspaper reports of the incident were scarce. The navy insisted there was no evidence of enemy aircraft. The US government continues to claim that the object was a weather balloon. Many people do not believe this argument. The mystery of the object in the sky over Los Angeles may never be solved.

Flying Saucers Sighted Over Mount Rainier

On June 24, 1947, former World War II pilot Kenneth Arnold spotted something strange above Washington's Mount Rainier. Arnold was flying at an altitude of 9,200 feet (2,800 m). Then a bright light startled him. At first, all he saw was a distant *DC-4* aircraft. Seconds later, Arnold saw nine objects flying diagonally between his airplane and Mount Rainier. He ruled out several possible explanations. It

Kenneth Arnold (center) looks at a photo of a UFO that he spotted.

1,700
Speed, in miles per hour (2,736 km/h), that Arnold estimated the disks were traveling.

- Kenneth Arnold was a former World War II pilot.
- He saw nine disks flying diagonally above Mount Rainier in Washington on June 24, 1947.
- Similar sightings were reported after Arnold's account.
- Arnold's sighting coined the term "flying saucer."

was not reflections from his windows. The objects' estimated speed also meant it was not a flock of geese.

Arnold concluded what he saw was most likely military aircraft. They were performing experimental flight operations. The army denied this. They claimed that Arnold was seeing things. The publicity surrounding Arnold's account sparked similar sightings. Someone on nearby Mount Adams reported seeing the same objects at about the same time. A United Airlines crew claimed to have seen nine flying disks of the same shape and size. They saw them above Idaho ten days after Arnold's sighting.

Arnold saw the mysterious objects near Mount Rainier in Washington.

The disks Arnold saw in the sky soon became the first widely reported unidentified flying objects (UFOs) in US history. Arnold's description of the disks even led to the introduction of the term "flying saucer."

UFO Crashes on New Mexico Ranch

It is the most well-known story in all of UFO history. It has sparked many people to question whether there is other life in space. But what really landed outside the town of Roswell, New Mexico, in July 1947? It is a mystery that has been fueling imaginations for years.

On the morning of July 3, rancher William "Mac" Brazel discovered the remains of a crashed aircraft in his sheep pasture. The night before, Brazel had heard what he thought was an explosion during a storm.

Members of the military identify pieces of a weather balloon found near Roswell.

75
Distance, in miles (120 km), from Roswell to Brazel's ranch.

- Strange aircraft pieces were found in a sheep pasture at Brazel's ranch on July 3, 1947.
- The military took the debris away under heavy guard.
- The air force claimed the aircraft was a weather balloon.
- Some stories claim that aliens were taken from the crash site.

Now the town of Roswell has many shops and museums about UFOs and aliens.

Brazel called the Roswell police because the aircraft looked unusual. The Roswell sheriff told the nearby US Army Air Force base about the accident. Soon, soldiers collected the crashed craft. The aircraft was quickly taken away in large, armored trucks.

The air force base's commander claimed the military had a flying saucer. The following day, the base said it was a weather balloon. Many witnesses claimed the debris looked nothing like a weather balloon. It

THINK ABOUT IT

The Roswell accident made aliens a part of popular culture. Why is that? What part of the incident sparked people's imaginations? Name three movies or books where aliens play a major role.

was later released that the debris was part of a top-secret project.

Additional stories include one that claims that aliens were recovered from the crash. Some believe aliens are being kept at a top-secret military base known as Area 51. NASA and the US military have denied this claim.

4

Unexplained Lights Lead to Photographs

On the night of August 25, 1951, three professors from the Texas Technological College stood outside talking. Suddenly, a series of bright lights flashed across the sky above Lubbock, Texas. The lights formed a crescent. A moment later, they made a second pass across the sky. The professors checked with the US Air Force the next day. They determined that no planes had flown over the area at the time of the sighting.

The photos taken by Carl Hart Jr. were reprinted across the United States, making the UFO sighting famous.

50

Number of lights seen in the sky above Lubbock.

- Three professors saw unexplained crescents of light in the sky on August 25, 1951.
- Eighteen-year-old Carl Hart Jr. snapped photos of the lights on August 30.
- Hart's photos were published in numerous papers and magazines, including *Life*.
- No true explanation has ever been given about the objects in Hart's photos.

FILM INSPIRATION

Six years after the Lubbock Lights, the nearby town of Levelland, Texas, had 15 reports in one night about a UFO. Witnesses reported that a torpedo-shaped, illuminated object passed cars and trucks. It caused their engines and headlights to temporarily die. The incident is reported to be a possible inspiration for the 1977 Steven Spielberg film, *Close Encounters of the Third Kind*.

This was the first of many sightings in the area. Between August and November 1951, the professors noted 12 different sightings. Many other people in and around Lubbock also saw the crescents arcing through the night sky.

Five days after the initial sighting, 18-year-old Carl Hart Jr. saw white lights flying in a *V* formation out his window. Hart slipped out to the backyard and snapped five different exposures of the lights. He took photos over the course of five hours. Hart's photos show between 18 and 20 objects in crescent formations. The *Lubbock Avalanche-Journal* paid Hart $10 to print his photos. They were soon reprinted in newspapers and magazines around the country, including *Life*.

The Lubbock Lights were one of the most-published events in the history of UFOs. The US Air Force concluded the lights were neither birds nor alien spacecraft. However, no explanation has ever been given about what was flying above Lubbock that year.

Aliens Visit Washington, DC

"Jets Chase DC Sky Ghosts." That was the headline across the front page of the *Washington Daily News* on July 26, 1952. The night before, mysterious lights had buzzed across the skies of Washington, DC. But no one knew the true source of the lights.

The mysterious lights over DC began on July 19. Air traffic controllers at Washington National Airport and Andrews Air Force Base saw a cluster on their radar screens. The airport control tower sent a message to commercial flights, asking if anyone could confirm the lights. Captain S. C. "Casey" Pierman of Capital Air Flight 807 responded. He saw six bright lights that looked similar to falling stars. Witnesses on the ground also saw the strange lights. Fighter jets were sent into

7

Number of initial lights discovered on the air traffic control radar screen.

- Commercial pilot Casey Pierman spied strange lights in the air on July 19, 1952.
- One week later, the lights returned.
- A US Air Force pilot intercepted the crafts, but they disappeared.
- Skeptics believe that the lights were new fighter jets or missiles.

THINK ABOUT IT

Have you ever seen strange lights in the night sky? Name three things you would find lighting up the sky at night.

The mysterious lights passed over the Capitol, as well as the White House and the Pentagon.

the sky to stop the crafts. But the pilots saw nothing.

The lights returned the following weekend. They moved in unpredictable patterns. They were traveling at speeds of roughly 900 miles per hour (1,450 km/h). Jets once again scrambled into the sky. The pilots could see the bright lights speeding away from them. One pilot observed the lights from 10 miles (16 km) away as they turned and began to dart in his direction. The pilot radioed Andrews Air Force Base, asking if he should open fire. Then the lights disappeared.

Some believe that the lights were new fighter jets or missiles. Other people think the lights were caused by hot weather. The official US Air Force report calls the lights "unknowns." The source of them remains unknown to this day.

Aliens Abduct New Hampshire Couple

Barney and Betty Hill were driving to New Hampshire from a brief vacation in Canada on September 19, 1961. Sometime around 10:15 p.m., Barney saw a brightly lit craft shaped similar to a pancake. Flashing lights covered the ship. Barney saw several aliens staring out at him from the ship as it got closer. The Hills left the wooded road quickly. However, they soon realized that they were further along on their trip than they thought they should be. Hours had passed without their knowing.

Betty and Barney Hill were driving on dark, wooded roads when they saw a bright light and a ship.

TAKEN BY ALIENS

In November 1975, a team of loggers was returning home from work in an Arizona forest. They spied a glowing, flattened disk hovering over a dirt road. One of the workers, Travis Walton, approached the object and disappeared. He turned up five days later with vague memories of being abducted by aliens. His story was told in the book *Fire in the Sky*, which later became a movie.

2

Number of hours unaccounted for on the night the Hills saw the UFO.

- On September 19, 1961, the Hills saw a craft in the sky.
- The local air force base confirmed the sighting of an unexplained object.
- Betty had terrible nightmares.
- Under hypnosis, Barney and Betty told stories of being abducted by aliens.

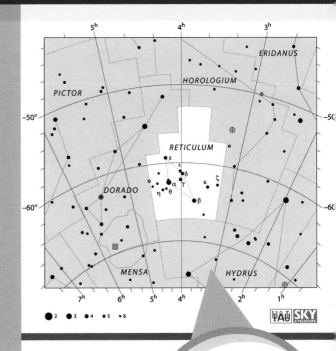

Other things puzzled them after their return home. Betty's dress was torn and stained. Barney's shoes were scuffed. Their watches had stopped. Betty phoned her close friend at the nearby Pease Air Force Base. She reported the mysterious object. He told her the base's radar had also seen a UFO at that time.

Betty's nightmares began ten days later. Two years after the nightmares, the Hills were placed under hypnosis. They recalled being taken aboard the alien's ship. Barney and Betty described the aliens as being bald, having grayish skin, and standing about 5 feet (1.5 m) tall. Betty also remembered being shown something similar to a star map. Under hypnosis, Betty drew a star system known as Zeta Reticuli. While some claimed that the Hills made up the story, their tale never changed.

The stars in Zeta Reticuli can be seen in dark, southern skies without the use of a telescope.

Unknown Fireball Falls from the Sky

Dusk blanketed the quiet rural town of Kecksburg, Pennsylvania, on December 9, 1965. Suddenly, a giant fireball shot across the sky. According to a 14-year-old boy who was outside at the time, the object was the size of a full moon. It sparked bits of light before crashing into the woods. The fireball was seen in several states. Particles from the mysterious object were scattered for miles in every direction.

Witnesses to the fireball in Kecksburg claimed to have seen a copper-colored craft crash into the thick woods. Military vehicles rumbled into the peaceful town hours after its landing. Local firefighters attempted to reach the scene. They were turned away just 200 feet (61 m) from the crash site.

Bob Gatty, a reporter for the *Greensburg Tribune-Review,* drove to the woods. He was turned away and was told he would be arrested if he went any farther. Military officials covered the mysterious object in a tarp. They loaded it onto a flatbed truck and drove away.

While no images of the 1965 incident are available, it is possible the fireball looked similar to this.

15

Length, in feet (4.6 m), that the acorn-shaped craft was reported to be.

- Witnesses described a copper-colored ship crashing into the woods on December 9, 1965.
- The military removed the object.
- A firefighter claimed to have seen strange writing on the craft.
- One possible theory is that the craft was a Soviet satellite.

The case remained closed for many years. Then the television show *Unsolved Mysteries* ran a story on the incident. UFO specialists began to investigate it further. New information was released about the night of the crash. A photographer who snapped photos of the craft had them seized by the military, according to his widow. A witness at the time described writing on the craft that looked similar to Egyptian hieroglyphics. The mystery has never been solved. Some people believe the object was the Soviet satellite Cosmos 96. The Russians disagree, saying the technology was most likely American.

The mysterious object may have had writing on it that looked similar to hieroglyphics.

Future US President Carter Reports Strange Lights

Jimmy Carter stood outside on a cool January night in 1969. He saw a strange bright light above the town of Leary, Georgia. Carter was not the only one to spy the object as it hovered above the horizon. An estimated 10 to 12 people stood outside with Carter.

According to Carter, the object had no solid substance. It was just an odd light. It drew closer, then lessened, and stopped beyond a forest of pine trees. Then the light began to change colors. It changed from blue to red to white. Carter took out his tape recorder. He described what he saw so he could write it down later. A few years later, in September 1973, Carter filed a report about the sighting with the National Investigations Committee on Aerial Phenomena.

While campaigning for president in 1976, Carter vowed that, if elected, he would speak to the government about releasing UFO information to the public. However, after successfully winning the presidential election, he went back on his word.

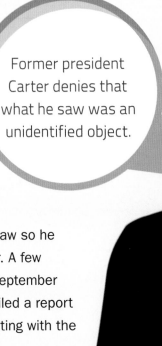

Former president Carter denies that what he saw was an unidentified object.

He claimed it was for the safety of the country.

The former president has since said he does not believe the light he saw belonged to an alien spacecraft. Some say the object was the planet Venus. Carter, an amateur astronomer, disputed this. He said he knew what Venus would have looked like that night.

Some people said Venus was near maximum brightness at the time in 1969.

7:15
Time of night when Carter alleged to have seen a UFO.

- Future president Jimmy Carter and others saw a bright light hover on the horizon in January 1969.
- Carter filed a UFO report in 1973.
- During his campaign for president, Carter vowed to release UFO information to the public.
- Carter later said the light did not belong to an alien spacecraft.

RONALD REAGAN

Jimmy Carter is not the only United States president to have seen a UFO. When he was governor of California in 1974, future president Ronald Reagan was on an airplane when a mysterious light appeared behind it. The light quickly sped off. Reagan retold his story to a man named Norman Miller. When he remembered that Miller was a reporter, he stopped speaking. Reagan never spoke publicly about his experience again.

19

Pilot's Strange Final Words Fuel UFO Mystery

Shortly after sunset on October 21, 1978, pilot Frederick Valentich was flying over Bass Strait toward King Island near Australia. Valentich's airplane soon encountered mysterious lights and disappeared without a trace.

As Valentich flew southeast, he saw what he assumed to be another airplane pass over him. He radioed Melbourne Airport to ask if any large aircraft was known to be at the same altitude. None was. He spoke with air traffic controllers for at least six minutes while he trailed the strange lights.

Valentich described the aircraft as long and traveling straight for him. Then he said the aircraft was hovering above his plane. He said it was shiny with a green light. Valentich's engine began to cough. Then air traffic control heard his final message: "It is not an aircraft."

The transmission was followed by open static. Valentich had vanished. A wide search was carried out, but no trace of his plane was found.

20
Age of Frederick Valentich when he disappeared.

- Valentich flew over the Bass Strait on October 21, 1978.
- He followed four strange lights that formed a long shape.
- He spoke with air traffic control for at least six minutes.
- Valentich's final transmission before disappearing was, "It is not an aircraft."

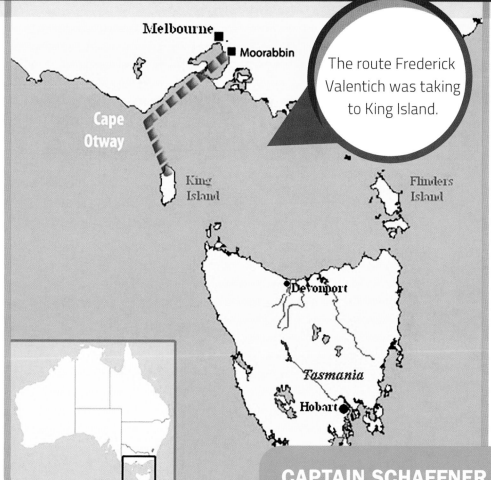

The route Frederick Valentich was taking to King Island.

Some people thought he faked his own death. A 315-page file said pieces of wreckage believed to be from Valentich's plane were recovered in Bass Strait. But they could not confirm that they belonged to the missing plane. To this day, Valentich's disappearance and haunting last words remain unexplained.

CAPTAIN SCHAFFNER

During the Cold War, Captain William Schaffner intercepted an unknown aircraft over the North Sea. The experienced pilot disappeared from radar. While his plane was eventually found, Schaffner's body was missing. Official reports say Schaffner's plane crashed because he was flying low. Many UFO believers claim he was abducted.

Diamond-Shaped UFO Sickens Eyewitnesses

On December 29, 1980, Betty Cash, Vickie Landrum, and Vickie's seven-year-old grandson Colby were driving home. Cash was behind the wheel when she spied a distant light up ahead. Moments later, the light became a towering ship in front of them. The ship shot out flames and made a beeping sound.

The three passengers got out of the car. They stood on the side of the road before the diamond-shaped ship. As they watched, a swarm of helicopters surrounded the ship. The UFO lifted into the air, followed by the helicopters.

After returning home, Cash, Landrum, and Colby began to suffer odd effects. They were vomiting and had a burning sensation in their eyes. They also felt as if they were sunburned. A few days later, Cash's symptoms grew worse. She lost portions of her hair and skin. She suffered from large blisters. She could not walk at all.

A radiologist examined the three and determined they had secondary radiation damage. The trio attempted

ALIEN ENCOUNTERS

US astronomer and UFOlogist J. Allen Hynek developed a classification system for encounters with aliens. The first stage is a UFO sighting at 500 feet (152 m) or less. The sighting of a UFO with physical effects is the second stage. The third stage involves seeing an alien. Being abducted by aliens is the fourth and final stage.

to sue the US government. They claimed the government was responsible for the UFO and the leaked radiation. It was a rare example of a criminal case involving UFOs. The case was thrown out.

Number of helicopters surrounding the unknown craft.

- Betty Cash and Vickie and Colby Landrum saw the spacecraft on December 29, 1980.
- Helicopters surrounded it before it fell away.
- The three witnesses grew sick after returning home.
- Doctors determined they had radiation poisoning.

The only public statement from the military about the activity in the Texas woods that evening came from Fort Hood. The military base said no Fort Hood aircraft were in the area that night.

Vickie Landrum speaks with the media after seeing a possible UFO.

Mysterious Object Over Turkey Filmed

Some have called videos captured by Yeni Kent Compound night guard Yalcin Yalman the most important UFO videos. Shot in Istanbul, Turkey, between 2007 and 2009, the nighttime footage showed shaky images of what appeared to be an unknown craft. Many people saw the disk-shaped object around the time when Yalman filmed it.

In the time-stamped footage, a curved, metallic oval hovered and moved silently. Red and orange lights glowed brightly from time to time. In part of the video, it even appeared as if two aliens could be seen within the ship.

Sirius UFO Space Sciences Research Center is Turkey's primary UFO reporting organization. The center and two other organizations examined hours of footage to determine if it was fake. They looked

35
Length, in minutes, of the examined recordings.

- Night watchman Yalcin Yalman videotaped bright lights on many occasions between 2007 and 2009.
- The hovering objects were curved and metallic.
- A UFO research center determined the images on the video were not faked.
- Skeptics claim the images were created using computer animation.

THINK ABOUT IT

Technology is helpful in capturing possible proof of UFOs. It can also be used to create believable hoaxes. Why is this? Find examples of how technology has been used to create fake stories about aliens.

Was it possible there were UFOs above the compound in Turkey?

at the time stamp and date on each of the videos. They also looked at the moon phases. The altitude of the craft was compared to the horizon line.

The three organizations concluded the footage was not created using computer animation, video special effects, or models and wires. They believed it was possible that as many as three different crafts were recorded. Despite this, Turkish scientists claimed the UFO was created using computer animation.

Disk-Shaped Objects Hover Over England

Steve Lambert was leaving the Running Horse restaurant in Bracknell, England, in June 2013, to make a phone call. Dusk was settling on the overcast sky. But as Lambert looked up, two disk-shaped objects glimmered in the sky. Lambert quickly used his phone's camera to take a picture of the fast-moving crafts. Lambert had time to take only one photo before they disappeared.

But one photo was enough. It was called one of the best photos taken in

Lambert was able to capture one photo of the mysterious disks before they disappeared.

UFO history by Nick Pope. Pope worked for the British Ministry of Defence.

Lambert's sighting was not the only one in the area. In February 2013, just two miles (3.2 km) from the Bracknell sighting, there was also a sighting.

Many people share the enthusiasm of Lambert and others

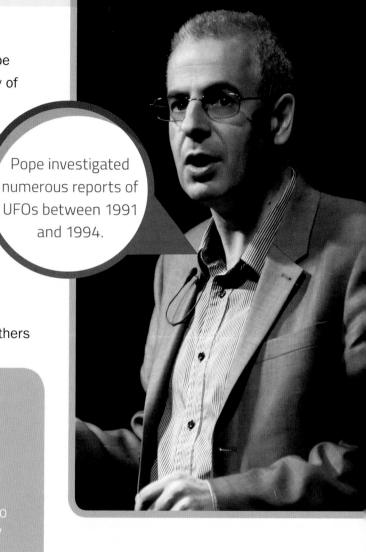

Pope investigated numerous reports of UFOs between 1991 and 1994.

4
Number of seconds Lambert saw the mysterious craft.

- Steve Lambert saw two disk-shaped objects fly over Running Horse in Bracknell, England, in June 2013.
- Lambert captured the objects in a photograph on his phone.
- An ex-Ministry of Defence official claimed that Lambert's photo was one of the best he had seen.
- Other sightings occurred nearby.

who saw the two crafts. Some skeptics are certain that what he saw could easily be explained. The owner of the Running Horse said the fast-moving craft were airplanes and nothing more. Still, the mystery remains. What were the two streaks of light across the skies of Bracknell?

27

Fact Sheet

- Many civilizations, including the ancient Sumerians and Egyptians, may have symbols of UFOs in their written languages.

- The first official written report of a UFO sighting came from former British Prime Minister Winston Churchill, who claimed to have seen a strange airship on October 14, 1912, in Kent, England.

- On October 30, 1938, a radio dramatization of H. G. Wells' popular novel *The War of the Worlds* was broadcast. Many believed that the radio show's fake news bulletins were real, leading to a mass panic.

- Since the 1940s, there have been thousands of UFO sightings. In fact, the US government once had a division assigned to investigate them. It was called Project Blue Book.

- Alongside UFOs, many claim to have also been visited by Men in Black, groups of up to three individuals wearing black suits who visit recent UFO witnesses. They claim to represent a government agency. People who encounter the Men in Black often feel ill for days afterward.

- To this day, sightings of strange lights and aircraft continue to occur frequently. Some, however, are hoaxes or are easily explained. For example, a UFO seen flying over London, England, during the Olympics opening ceremony's fireworks was later discovered to be a Goodyear blimp flying without signage.

Glossary

altitude
The height of an airplane above sea level.

astronomer
A person who is a specialist in the science of things outside Earth's atmosphere.

horizon
The line where the earth or sea seems to meet the sky.

hypnosis
A sleep-like state in which a person can hear and respond to questions.

intercept
To stop and take something before it reaches its intended destination.

skeptic
A person who questions or doubts something.

transmission
The process of sending electrical signals to a radio.

UFOlogist
A person who studies unidentified flying objects.

For More Information

Books

Bringle, Jennifer. *Alien Sightings in America*. New York: Rosen, 2012.

Hile, Lori. *Aliens and UFOs*. Chicago: Raintree, 2014.

Kincade, Chris. *Encountering Aliens: Eyewitness Accounts*. North Mankato, MN: Capstone, 2015.

Shea, Therese. *Investigating UFOs and Aliens*. New York: Britannica, 2015.

Visit 12StoryLibrary.com

Scan the code or use your school's login at **12StoryLibrary.com** for recent updates about this topic and a full digital version of this book. Enjoy free access to:

- Digital ebook
- Breaking news updates
- Live content feeds
- Videos, interactive maps, and graphics
- Additional web resources

Note to educators: Visit 12StoryLibrary.com/register to sign up for free premium website access. Enjoy live content plus a full digital version of every 12-Story Library book you own for every student at your school.

Index

About the Author

Brandon Terrell is a Minnesota-based writer. He is the author of numerous children's books, including picture books, chapter books, and graphic novels. Terrell enjoys watching movies and television, reading, playing baseball, and spending every moment with his wife and their two children.

READ MORE FROM 12-STORY LIBRARY

Every 12-Story Library book is available in many formats. For more information, visit 12StoryLibrary.com.